The best
GOLf
jOKeS

Published in the UK by
LITTLE **BLACK**DOG LIMITED
Unit 3 Everdon Park
Heartlands Business Park
NN11 8YJ

Telephone   01327 871 777
Facsimile   01327 879 222
E Mail   info@littleblackdogltd.co.uk

ISBN 13: 9781904967774

Printed and bound in China by 1010 International

A woman out golfing hits her ball into the woods.

She goes into the woods to look for it and finds a frog in a trap.

The frog said to her, "If you release me from this trap, I will grant you 3 wishes." The woman freed the frog and the frog said, "Thank you, but I failed to mention that there was a condition to your wishes - that whatever you wish for, your husband will get 10 times more or better!"

The woman said, "That would be OK," and for her first wish, she wanted to be the most beautiful woman in the world. The frog warned her, "You do realise that this wish will also make your husband the most handsome man in the world, an Adonis." The woman replied, "That's OK because I will be the most beautiful woman and he will only have eyes for me." So, KAZAM - she's the most beautiful woman in the world!

For her second wish, she wanted to be the richest woman in the world. The frog said, "That will make your husband the richest man in the world, 10 times richer than you." The woman said, "That's OK because what is mine is his and what is his is mine." So, KAZAM she's the richest woman in the world!

The frog then inquired about her third wish, and she answered, "I'd like a mild heart attack."

And for the male readers: The man had a heart attack ten times milder than his wife.

The moral of the story: Women are really dumb but think they're really smart.

PS: If you are a woman and are still reading this; it only goes to show that women never listen... now run along and put the kettle on, there's a love.

What's the difference between a bad golfer and a bad sky diver?
A bad golfer goes - whack, "oh shit!"
A bad sky diver goes "OH Shit!" whack.

Several men are in the changing room of a golf club.

A mobile phone on a bench rings and a man engages the hands free speaker function and began to talk. Everyone in the room stops to listen.

MAN: 'Hello'

WOMAN: 'Darling, it's me. Are you at the club?'

MAN: 'Yes'

WOMAN: 'I'm at the shopping centre and I've found this beautiful leather coat. It's only £1,000. Is it ok to buy it?'

MAN: 'Sure, go ahead if you like it that much.'

WOMAN: 'I also stopped by Mercedes dealership and saw the latest models. I saw one I really liked.'

MAN: 'How much?'

WOMAN: '£70,000'

MAN 'Ok, but for that price it should come with all the options.'

WOMAN: 'Great! Oh, one more thing... The house I wanted last year is back on the market. They're asking £950,000.'

MAN: 'Well, then go ahead and give them an offer of £900,000. They will probably take it. If not, you can go the extra 50 thousand. It really is a good price.'

WOMAN: 'Ok. I'll see you later! I love you so much!!'

MAN: 'Bye! I love you too.'

The man hangs up. The other men in the changing room are staring at him in astonishment, mouths agape...

He smiles and asks: 'Anyone know who this phone belongs to???'

Fred and George step up to the first tee, one said to the other, "Hey guess what, I got a set of golf clubs for my wife." To which the other replies, "What a great swap!"

On a golf tour in Ireland, Tiger Woods drives his BMW into a petrol station in a remote part of the countryside.

The pump attendant greets him in typical Irish manner completely unaware of who the golfer is. "Top of the mornin' to yer, sir," says the attendant. Tiger nods a quick "hello" and bends forward to pick up the nozzle.

As he does so, two tees fall out of his shirt pocket onto the ground. "What are dey den, son?" asks the attendant. "They're called tees" replies Tiger. "Well, what on de good earth are dey for?" inquires the Irishman. " They're for resting my balls on when I'm driving," says Tiger. " Feckin Jaysus," says the Irishman, "Dem boys at BMW tink of everything!"

Bill came home from golfing well after dark, his wife asked why he had been gone so long. He told her that after his 8.00 am round of golf he helped a beautiful blond change her flat tyre. She invited him back to hers for a drink and they ended up spending the afternoon in bed.

"Your a liar" she said you played 36 holes didn't you.

A fanatical golfer has an early tee time every Saturday and golfs all day long. One Saturday, he gets up early, dresses quietly, gets his clubs out of the closet, and goes out to his car to drive to the course.

There is a torrential downpour. It is snowing and raining and the wind is blowing at 50mph. He comes back into the house and turns the TV to the weather channel and finds it's going to be bad all day. So he puts his clubs back into the closet, quietly undresses and slips back into bed where he cuddles up to his wife's back, and whispers, "The weather out there is terrible." To which she replies, "Can you believe my stupid husband is out golfing?"

Why do golfers always carry two pairs of trousers?

In case they get a hole in one.

An Englishman, American, and Arabian were in a bar talking about their families. The Englishman said, "I have 10 kids at home and if I had another one I would have a soccer team!" "Well," said the American guy, "I have 15 kids at home and if I had another one I would have a football team!" "Well," said the Arabic guy, "I have 17 wives at home and if I had another one I would have a golf course."

A golfer stood over his tee shot for what seemed an eternity. Looking up, looking down, measuring the distance, figuring the wind direction and speed. He was driving his partner mad. Finally his exasperated partner says, "What's taking so long? Hit the blasted ball!" The guy answers, "My wife is up there watching me from the clubhouse. I want to make this a perfect shot." "Forget it, man, you'll never hit her from here!"

John's just about to set off on a round of golf when he realises that he forgot to tell his wife that the guy who fixes the washing machine is coming at noon.

So John heads back to the clubhouse and phones home.

"Hello?" says a little girl's voice. "Hi, honey, it's Daddy," says John. "Is Mummy near the phone?" "No, Daddy. She's upstairs in the bedroom with Uncle Fred."

After a brief pause, John says, "But you haven't got an Uncle Fred, honey!" "Yes, I do, and he's upstairs in the bedroom with Mummy!" "Okay, then, here's what I want you do. Put down the phone, run upstairs and knock on the bedroom door and shout to Mummy and Uncle Fred that my car's just pulled up outside the house."

"OK Daddy!" A few minutes later, the little girl comes back to the phone. "Well, I did what you said, Daddy." "And what happened?" "Well, Mummy jumped out of bed, ran around screaming, then tripped over the rug and went out the front window, and now she's dead." "Oh, my God! What about Uncle Fred?" "He jumped out of bed too, and he was all scared, and he jumped out the back window into the swimming pool. But he must have forgot that last week you took out all the water to clean it, so he hit the bottom of the swimming pool and now he's dead too."

There is a long pause. "Swimming pool? Is this 555-3097?"

An 85 year old couple, having been married almost 60 years, had died in a car crash. They had been in good health the last 10 years, mainly due to her interest in health food and exercise.

When they reached the pearly gates, St. Peter took them to their mansion which was equipped with a beautiful kitchen and luxury bathroom and jacuzzi. As they "oohed and aahed" the old man asked Peter how much all this was going to cost. "It's free," Peter replied, "this is Heaven."

Next they went out back to see the championship golf course that their home overlooked. They would have golfing privileges everyday and each week the course changed to a new one representing the great golf courses on earth. The old man asked, "What are the green fees?" Peter's reply, "This is heaven, you play free."

Next they went to the clubhouse and saw the lavish buffet lunch with the cuisine's of the world laid out. "How much to eat?" asked the old man.

"Don't you understand yet? This is heaven, it's free!" Peter replied. "Well, where are the low fat and low cholesterol foods?" the old man asked timidly.

"That's the best part... you can eat as much as you like of whatever you like and you never get fat and you never get sick. This is Heaven." The old man looked at his wife and said, "You and your f—king bran muffins. I could have been here 10 years ago!

Two friends were playing golf when one pulled out a cigar but he didn't have a lighter so he asked his friend if he had one. "I certainly do," he replied and reached into his golf bag and pulled out a 12 inch Bic lighter. "Wow!" said his friend, "Where did you get that monster?" "I got it from my genie."

"You have a genie?" he asked. "Yes, he's right here in my golf bag." "Could I see him?" He opens his golf bag and out pops the genie. The friend says, "I'm a good friend of your master. Will you grant me one wish?" "Yes," the genie said so he asks him for a million bucks and the genie hops back into the golf bag and leaves him standing there waiting for his million bucks.

Suddenly the sky begins to darken and there is the sound of a million ducks flying overhead. The friend tells his golfing partner, "I asked for a million bucks not ducks!" He answers, "I forgot to tell you the genie is hard of hearing. Do you really think I asked him for a 12 inch Bic?"

A foursome is waiting at the men's tee when another foursome of ladies are hitting from the ladies tee.

The ladies are taking their time and when finally the last one is ready to hit the ball she hacks it about 10 feet, goes over to it, hacks it another ten feet and looks up at the men waiting and says apologetically, "I guess all those f—king lessons I took this winter didn't help." One man immediately replies "No, you see that's your problem.... You should have been taking golf lessons instead."

Two guys are trying to get in a quick 18 holes, but there are two terrible lady golfers in front of them hitting the ball everywhere but where it's supposed to go.

The first guy says, "Why don't you go over and ask if we can play through?"

The second guy gets about halfway there, turns and comes back.

The first guy says, "What's wrong?" He says, "One of them is my wife, and the other is my mistress."

The first guy says, "That could be a problem. I'll go over." He gets about halfway there and he turns and comes back, too.

The second guy says, "What's wrong?"

The first guy says, "That's a coincidence!"

The first of two women tees off and watches in horror as her ball headed directly toward a foursome of men playing the next hole. The ball hits one of the men, and he immediately clasped his hands together at his crotch, fell to the ground and proceeded to roll around in agony.

The woman rushed down to the man and immediately began to apologise.

She explained that she was a physiotherapist: "Please allow me to help. I know I could relieve your pain if you'd just allow me!" she told him earnestly. "Ummph, oooh, nnooo, I'll be alright. I'll be fine in a few minutes," he replied breathlessly as he remained in the fetal position still clasping his hands at his crotch. But she persisted, and he finally allowed her to help him. She gently took his hands away and laid them to the side, she loosened his pants, and she put her hands inside. She began to massage his crotch. She then asked him: "How does that feel?" To which he replied: "It feels great. But my thumb still hurts like hell!"

What do golf and sex have in common?

They're two things you can enjoy even if you're bad at both.

What do you call a blonde golfer with an IQ of 125?

A foursome.

Bill's tee shot off the first tee hooks horribly and skips off the clubhouse roof. He decides it's not worth chasing so he tees up another ball and plays on. As he's making the turn at nine, his friend Little Johnny comes running out of the clubhouse, "Bill, wait!" "Yes, what is it?" "Did you see what happened to your ball from the first tee?" "Well, I hooked the ball off the clubhouse roof but I didn't see what happened to it." "Let me tell you, it ricocheted off a van's window which went out of control and hit a school bus. The bus tumbled down an embankment and burst into flames! Three kids are in critical condition at the hospital!" "Oh my God! What should I do?" "Well, I think if you just open your club face a little bit more . . ."

Tiger Woods is visiting a posh and popular southern states-area Country Club after winning the Masters Championship. He finds the front doors locked.

After ringing the ornate doorbell, a club member sticks his head out and looks Tiger up and down. "Can I help you?", he asks. Tiger replies, "Yes, I'd like to play a round of golf at your club."

The uppity club member shocks Tiger by saying: "Sorry, you can't play here. The club for your kind is about a 4 iron down the road." Angered almost beyond control, Tiger straightens his green jacket and screams, "But, I'm Tiger Woods, the 2008 US Open Champion!!!"

The man, obviously embarrassed, hits himself in the forehead and says, "Oh, Tiger Woods! I'm so sorry! It's only a 6 iron for you."

Aman is out playing golf and is having the round of his life. He comes up to the 17th hole, a long par 5 with a large oak tree in the middle of the fairway. He hits a beautiful tee shot down the left side of the fairway.

When he gets to his ball, he finds that there is one limb hanging over the fairway that may interfere with his 2nd shot. The man thinks to himself, "Do I pull out a 7 iron and play it safe or do I pull out the 3 wood and go for it?" The man has been having the best round of his life so decides to pull out the 3 wood. His second shot hits the overhanging limb, bounces straight back, striking him on the head and instantly kills him.

Now the man is at the Pearly Gates and is standing in front of Saint Peter. Saint Peter is looking in his book and can not seem to find the man's name. Finally, Saint Peter is so frustrated that he asks the man, "How did you get here?" The man replies, "I got here in two."

Jon comes to work speaking in a hoarse voice, His co-worker asked what happened and he explained about his round of golf the previous day. He took a really bad shot and sliced the ball out of bounds and into a pasture.

Whilst looking for the ball he meets a lady looking for her ball too. As he passes a cow he spots the ball stuck up it's backside, as he lifts the tail he calls to the lady and said, "Does this look like yours?" That's when she hit him in the throat with a 3 iron.

Three guys are golfing with the club pro. First guy tees off and hits a dribbler about 60 yards. He turns to the pro and says, "What did I do wrong?" The pro says, "Loft."

The next guy tees off and hits a duck hook into the woods. He asks the pro, "What did I do wrong?" The pro says, "Loft."

The third guy tees off and hits a slice into a pond. He asks the pro, "What did I do wrong?" The pro says, "Loft."

As they're walking to their balls, the first guy finally speaks up. He says to the pro, "The three of us hit completely different tee shots, and when we asked you what we did wrong you gave the same exact answer each time, 'What is loft?' " The pro says, "Lack of f——g talent."

A man slices his ball into the woods and goes in to look for it. He meets a girl from the next fairway looking for her ball. They start to chat and have a wonderful conversation. She suddenly says to him, "you know... you look like my third husband." He says, "Oh yes," and then asks her how many times she's been married. "Twice," she replies.

In primitive society, when native tribes beat the ground with clubs and yelled, it was called witchcraft; today, in civilised society, it is called golf.

One day the club's hacker challenges the pro to a match for £100.

The hacker told the pro that since he was much better than him, he must give the hacker two Gotchas'. The Pro had never heard of this but agreed anyway.

At the end of the match a few members gathered to watch the pro pay the hacker £100. A member asked the pro what had happened. The Pro said, 'I had to give him two Gotchas.' 'What the heck is that?' the member asked. 'Well I had the honour on the first tee and as I approached the ball and spread my feet to assume my stance he reached up and grabbed my balls as hard as he could and yelled Gotcha. Have you ever tried to play 18 holes waiting for the second Gotcha.'

Jesus, Moses and an old man were out golfing Jesus steps up to the tee and lets loose a power drive. The ball flies right over to the middle of a lake. Jesus walks over the water and hits his ball out of the water right onto the green.

Moses tees his ball up and he too unleashes one right into the lake. Moses walks up to the lake, parts the water, and chips his ball onto the green.

The old man steps up and he also blasts one out to the lake. Just as the ball is about to hit the water a fish jumps up and swallows the ball. Immediately an eagle swoops down and grabs the fish. As the eagle flies over the green the ball drops out of the fish's mouth, lands on the green and rolls into the cup.

Jesus says 'Come on Dad, stop messing around and play golf.'

A hack golfer spends a day at a smart country club, playing golf, enjoying the luxury of a complimentary caddy.

Being a hacker, he plays poorly all day. At the 18th, he spots a lake off to the left of the fairway.

He looks at the caddy and says, "I've played so poorly all day, I think I'm going to go drown myself in that lake. "The caddy looks back at him and says, "I don't think you could keep your head down that long."

A man goes for a quick round of golf, and at the first tee, someone is about to tee off in front of him.

The man takes a brand new ball out of his bag, unwraps it and places it on the tee. Thwack! Slices into the trees. "Boll–ks!" He reaches into his bag and takes out another brand new ball, unwraps it, and tees it up. Thwack! Hooks it miles into the bushes. "Boll–ks!"

He stomps back to his bag for another ball, when the man waiting approaches him. "Er, excuse me, but I notice you're losing a lot of brand new balls. Why don't you use an old one?" He looks at the man. "Because I've never bloody had one!"

A visiting golfer played 18 holes with his mates but needed to shower quickly before heading home. The men's locker room shower is full so his partners suggests he use the ladies showers as it was Saturday, a members only day. He had a great shower and just stepped out of the cubicle when three women walked into the locker room. Quick as a flash he retreated back into the shower. One woman whispered to the others, "Is that a man in our shower?". The woman asked her friends to kneel on the floor and look under the gap between the cubicle and the floor. The first woman looked and could only see the man from the waist down. She replied "that's not my husband." The second woman repeated the exercise, looked and replied "that's not my husband either." The third woman, a crusty old timer got down on her knees and peered under the wall, stood up and proudly reported, "He's not even a member at this club."

It was a Saturday morning, and Mike was beginning his pre-shot routine, visualising his upcoming shot when a voice came over the clubhouse loudspeaker- "Would the gentleman on the Ladies tee back up to the men's tee, please!"

Mike was still deep in his routine, seemingly impervious to the interruption. Again the announcement- "Would the MAN on the WOMEN'S tee kindly back up to the men's tee!"

Mike had had enough. He breaks his stance, lowers his driver back to the ground and shouts, "Would the announcer in the clubhouse kindly shut up and let me play my second shot?"

A blonde golfer goes into the pro shop and looks around frowning.

Finally the pro asks her what she wants.

"I can't find any green golf balls," the blonde replies. The pro looks all over the shop, and through all the catalogues, and finally calls the manufacturers and determines that sure enough, there are no green golf balls.

As the blonde golfer walks out the door in disgust, the pro asks her, "Before you go, could you tell me why you want green golf balls?"

"Well obviously, because they would be easier to find in the bunkers, stupid!!"

Paddy had such a bad round of golf he went home and beat his wife to death.

Feeling somewhat guilty he rang the police and said "I've just killed my wife". He gave the police his name and address and about a minute later a police car screeched up the driveway and two policeman got out and banged on the door.

Police: Are you the man who said he killed his wife?

Paddy: Yes, that was me.

Police: How did you kill her?

Paddy: I beat her to death with my one iron?

Police: How many times did you actually hit her?

Paddy: Er, Er, seven - but put me down for five.

Stevie Wonder and Jack Nicklaus are in a bar. Nicklaus turns to Wonder and says: "How is the singing career going?" Stevie Wonder says: "Not too bad, the latest album has gone into the top 10. By the way how is the golf." Nicklaus replies: "Not too bad, I am not winning as much as I used to but I'm still making money." Stevie Wonder says: "I find that when my swing goes wrong I need to stop playing for a while, then the next time I play it's alright." Jack Nicklaus says: "You play golf!" Stevie Wonder says: "Yes, have been for years." Nicklaus says: "But I thought you were blind, how can you play golf if you are blind?" He replies: "I get my caddie to stand in the middle of the fairway and he calls to me, I listen for the sound of his voice and play the ball towards him. Then when I get to where the ball lands the caddie moves further down the fairway or to the green and again I play the ball towards his voice."

"But how do you putt?" says Nicklaus. "Well,"

says Stevie, "I get my caddie to lean down in front of the hole and call to me with his head on the ground and I just play the ball towards the sound of his voice." Nicklaus says, "What's your handicap?" Stevie says: "I play off scratch." Nicklaus is incredulous and says to Stevie, "We must play a game..." Wonder replies, "Well, people don't take me seriously so I only play for money, and I never play for less than £100,000 a hole." Nicklaus thinks it over and says, "OK, I'm up for that - when would you like to play?" "Any night next week is OK with me."

At a posh club in Manila, a very arrogant and nasty American is playing a round with a client. He is very abusive to his caddy but all smiles with his client. You know the type.

At the sixth hole, 185yds over water, he demands of his caddy, "What club do I use here?" The caddy says, in broken English, "when Robert Duvall played here last year, he used a six iron." The golfer rudely grabs the six iron and hits the ball. the ball lands in the middle of the pond and the golfer erupts " hey stupid, you gave me a six iron and it was obviously not enough - I went right into the water!!" The caddy replies " that's what Robert Duvall did too."

Two blonde golfers in Ireland were on a very foggy par 3. They could see the top of the flag but not the green. Not to worry, their caddies said, they go up to the green and watch. So off they went. When they reached the green and looked around they found one ball 2 feet from the hole, the other in the hole. The caddies asked what ball they were using as they were unsure which one had holed out, both said they were using Maxfli 2 balls. All decided the only way to find a solution was to talk to the pro.

After hearing the story, seeing the balls, congratulating them for their great shots, he asked the caddies "OK, now which of them was using the orange ball?"

A beautiful, shapely young blonde arrives at her course alone and joins a threesome of men. All through the round with the help of tips from the 3 men she arrives at the 18th hole with her score on 98 and a 6-foot putt left to break 100. She tells the men "I have never broken 100 since I started playing golf. I am so anxious to break 100 that whichever one of you men gives me the best tip to sink this putt, I will reward him by making love to him right here on the green. So the first man checks the line and break from all sides and suggests she borrow 3 inches right of the hole and just stroke it hard enough to drop it in the hole. The second man agrees, but tells her to hit it firm and straight into the hole. She looks around for the third man and finds him frantically undressing right down to his birthday suit. She asks him what on earth he is doing. He replies he has won the love making session. She tells him he hasn't even given her his tip. To this he replies " Pick it up, it's a gimmee"

As normal, Mum was waiting for her 10 year old son to finish his Sunday tournament. When he finally finished and came to the club house he was absolutely filthy and covered in slime. His Mum yelled at him "Tommy, what have you been doing?" Tommy replied "Mum, when we were passing the stream on the 17th we bombed some frogs with balls then put firecrackers up their arses". The horrified Mum said. "Tommy, it's rectum." Tommy came back, "Sure did Mum!"

A Jewish man went to a golf course where they advertised they could provide a caddies of all types, so he asked the Caddy Master for a caddy who could work Jewish style. This surprised the Caddy master, he had never had such a request before - Lefties, half blind, lame, slicers, yes, but never Jewish. Nevertheless, he called the boys and asked if anybody could help out. After a long silence, a new caddy sitting in the corner said he could.

On the way to the first tee the boy said, "I really do not know how to caddy Jewish style, but being new I wanted to impress the other boys. So if you show me how, I will do it for half price." The man replied, "You learn fast..."

An 8 year-old boy and his 6 year-old brother were playing golf with their friends and practising both their game and their swearing. The older boy suggests after the game it is time they introduce their parents to their new talent. He tells his little brother, "When we go back to the clubhouse I'll say 'hell' and you say 'ass'." The 6 year-old readily agrees. As the two boys are seating themselves in the club house for snacks their mother comes and asks how the game went. The 8 year-old replies, "Hell, Mum, it was good except I got a triple bogie".

The surprised mother reacts with a swift whack on the boy's bottom and tells him to go to the car. The boy runs off crying and rubbing his backside.

With a sterner voice, the mother asks her younger son how his game was. The boy replies, "Ok, but you can bet your ass I didn't get a triple bogie!"

A young executive was asked by his boss to take some out of town visitors to a golf day. The man was delighted, played 18 holes with the guests, had a few beers and laughs with the waiter in the clubhouse, said goodbye, then rushed home.

When he got home to tell his wife the good news all was quiet. When he opened the bedroom door, alas, he found his wife in bed with his boss.

He left, went back to the course, into the bar, and the waiter said "I thought you went home". The man explained, "Yes, I went home, found my wife in bed with my boss. As they were in the early stages I thought I might be able to fit in another nine."

Two couples play golf together regularly at their club, and on the sixth hole, a par four, the second shot to the green must carry 80 yards over water.

One of the women, Mrs Smith, for over a year, could never carry the water, and would always hit into it, totally psyched out by the presence of the water.

Her friend suggested a hypnotist might help. The hypnotist planted the suggestion that when playing the second shot on the sixth hole, she would not see water, but rather a lush green fairway leading all the way up to the green.

About six months later, someone at the club asked whatever happened to Mrs. Smith, as she hadn't seen her playing for months now. She was informed that five months earlier, Mrs. Smith had drowned at the par four sixth!!!

Three golfers are standing at the gates of heaven and St Peter asked them if they ever cheated while playing golf with their wives.

The first man said, "all the time," so St. Peter gave him a motorcycle and admitted him to heaven.

The second man said, "I cheated a couple of times," so St Peter gave him a mid-sized car and let him into heaven.

The third man said, "For 40 years I only ever played golf with my wife. Most of the time she beat me but I never cheated." So St. Peter gave him a Rolls-Royce and admitted him to heaven.

A week later the three men met at an intersection in heaven and the third man was sitting in his car crying. The other men asked why he was crying, after all, he had such a nice car. The third man said "I just saw my wife and she was riding a skateboard."

Two friends are playing golf together. One of them has landed on a dirt track, covered in gravel and sunken stones. The owner of the ball ask his friend: " Do you mind if I have a drop, I cannot play from here, it's too rough." "No, I'm sorry, you play from where you lie!" " But I'm going to destroy the club, it's all rocks and gravel." "Tough, but no favours, you play from where you lie."   The poor chap stops arguing and take his first trial swing and of course, gravel and sparks fly everywhere. Second swing, same again. Finally he feels ready, moves to the ball and hits ... gravel and sparks everywhere, but the ball flies off beautifully, lands on the green and stops inches from the cup. " My God, what a shot!... which club did you use?"   "Your five iron."

A lady newcomer to golf was having a lesson on the first tee and asked the pro "What do I do now?" The pro replied, "Well, see that flag on the green, you have to hit your ball as close to it as you can." The lady let fly with a mighty swipe, the ball went flying and came to rest 3 inches from the hole. She asked "What do I do now?". The pro answered "You hit it into the hole." The woman screamed... "why didn't you tell me that in the first place."

One Sunday a usually happy weekend golfer came home from the game very late, and much the worse for wear. His wife greeted him at the door and demanded, "Where the hell have you been. What have you been doing?" The husband wobbled around and slurred "Had a bad game, sort of lost everything... you had better pack some bags I even lost you." The wife screamed "How could you do that?" The man replied, "It wasn't easy, I had to miss 3 one-foot putts in the last 4 holes."

The manager of a bank noticed that a co-member at his golf club would come to the bank every Monday morning and deposit £10,000. This went on week after week and it aroused the manager's curiosity.

The next Sunday he saw the man near the first tee with a few Chinese guests and approached him. The manager commented, "I notice that every Monday morning you come to my bank and deposit £10,000. You must have a very reliable business. May I ask what it is?" The man replied, "Oh, I'm a gambler." The manager asked, "You must be good, or have a special system. I didn't think you could win that much on the golf course." The man came back, "I do not really bet on golf. A lot of people come here who will bet on anything. For example.... I will bet you £10,000 that by bank opening on Monday your testicles will be square." The manager had never heard anything so crazy and immediately accepted the bet. Rubbing his hands in anticipation he

55

went off for his game, but all day kept putting his hands in his pocket to check out his equipment. Game over, he went home, had a bath, and was happy to see all was normal. The next morning he set off for the bank early, still satisfied all was OK, waited, and 10 minutes before opening the gambler came along with an old Chinese man. The manager, smiling, let him in and advised, "You owe me £10,000. They are still round." The man said "OK, no problem, but I am sure you will not mind if I check." The manager did not hesitate, so the gambler undid his fly, slid his hand in and checked his things. At that moment the Chinese man collapsed on the floor. "My God, what is wrong with your friend" queried the Manager. "Nothing really" answered the man, "it's just I bet him £20,000 I could play with the bank Managers balls before opening on Monday."

A husband and wife team played golf together every day and the wife was always beating the husband. Tired of this humiliation, the husband decides one day to break his wife concentration . He goes up to her as she was ready to tee off and says

" Honey, I love you more then anything in the world, that's why I must be honest with you, I had a mistress for the 15 years we have been married.

Of course, that day, the wife could not hit a good shot and lost the game to her husband for the first time in their married life.

The next day, the wife decides it is also time to be truthful to her husband.

As he was ready to tee off she says, "Honey, since you were so true to me yesterday, I feel obliged to do the same...before we met, I was a man...Well you can imagine the husband's golf that day. The next morning at the office, the poor husband is broken down...can't get over what his wife told him...his fellow worker notices his state of mind and asks what's wrong...the husband tells the story, still very troubled by it...."Well, says the co-worker, forget about that, you love your wife, you have been happy for 15 years, get over it and go on as if she had never told you." "That's not the point" answers the husband...she has been playing off the women's tee for all that time!!

My wife asked me why I don't play golf with Jerry anymore. I asked her "would you continue to play with a man who always gets drunk, loses so many balls, is always letting other groups play through, tells lousy jokes while you are trying to putt and generally offends everyone around him on the course?" "Certainly not, dear" she replied. "Well, neither would he."

A couple of friends were playing a round on a remote course in the tropics of Northern Australia.

After a few holes one of them needed to relieve himself, so he walked into the rough, dropped out his thing and began to pee. Alas, as he was in mid-stride, an enormous snake slid up and bit his thing.

The man screamed for help. His friend rushed over and was asked to find help quickly.

So his friend ran back to the clubhouse, saw the doctor, and asked what could be done.

The doctor told him to treat snake bites you have to make a small cut where the bite is, then suck it until all the poison comes out.

He thanked the doctor and ran back to his friend who asked, "What did the doctor say?" His friend replied, "You're going to die."

One day three elderly golfers were having their weekly round when the 60 year old said, "Well, life sure gets tough when you get on in years." His 70 year old companion asked what he meant. The younger man said, "well, every day I wake up at 6am and want a pee, however, no matter how I try it won't come." The 70 year old finished putting, thought and said, "Man, you got it easy, every day I wake at 6am and want a poo. No matter how I grunt and strain, no luck. Even medicine doesn't work."

There older partner, an 80 year old who had been quietly listening advised, "Your both lucky, my problems are much worse. One of the men asked how come and he replied, "Every day I pee at 6am and every day I poo at 6.05am." His friends looked at him and ask "how can that be so bad." The older man replied, "I don't wake up until 6.30am."

One Sunday a group of 8 year old golfers were playing when one of the girls hit her ball OB, into an adjoining house. One of the boys ran off to get it for her, over the fence, across the road, up the steps, and on to the veranda.

As he went to pick up the ball he noticed a condom. He went running back with the ball and said to the girl "hey, there's a condom on the veranda".........she replied........"what's a veranda?"

A really rich Texas oil man had his own golf course built on his property.

Not being a great golfer he only used it when he had guests.

One day on the first hole a guest asked, "What is par for this hole?" The Texan replied, "you set par at anything you want, last week I set it at 10.... and I made a birdie....."

Four golfers met at a golf course and were discussing how they persuaded their wives to let them play golf.

The first golfer said that he sent his wife a dozen red roses and cooked a gourmet dinner for two.

The second golfer said that he did all the vacuuming, dusting and laundry.

The third golfer said that he painted the kitchen so that his wife would let him play. The fourth golfer said he set the alarm for 5.30am and then he would wake up, roll over, and ask his wife "Intercourse or Golf course?" and his wife replied "Don't forget your sweater."

During the Ladies monthly tournament one woman hit a really bad slice, so bad it crossed the stream alongside the hole. She saw where the ball landed, and not wanting to lose it called to a blonde walking near where it landed, "How do I get to the other side?" The blonde looked across at her a bit confused and called back "What do you mean, you are already on the other side!"

There was this preacher who was an avid golfer. Every chance he could get, he could be found on the golf course. It was an obsession.

One Sunday was a perfect day for golfing. The preacher was in a quandary as to what to do, and shortly, the urge to play golf overcame him. He called an assistant to tell him that he was sick and could not do church.

He packed the car, and drove three hours to a golf course where no one would recognise him. Happily, he began to play the course and an angel up above was watching him, quite perturbed. He went to God and said, "Look at the preacher. He should be punished for what he is doing." God nodded in agreement. The preacher teed up on the first hole. He swung at the ball, and it sailed effortlessly through the air and landed right in the cup 350 yards away - a perfect hole-in-one. He was amazed and excited.

The angel was a little shocked. He turned to God

and said, "Begging your pardon, but I thought you were going to punish him." God smiled. "Think about it - who can he tell?"

They stood at the altar, waiting to be married. The bride-to-be looked down and saw a set of golf clubs beside her new husband's feet. "What on earth are you doing with those golf clubs?" she whispered.

"Well," he said, "This won't take all afternoon will it?"

In a group of golfers playing together Tom plays brilliantly, finishing three under.

Next weekend the foursome goes out again and once more Tom shoots a great round, but the others notice that this time he has played left-handed instead of right-handed as he had the week before.

The following two weeks it's the same story, left or right handed Tom plays a great round. Finally, one of the others has to ask him, "how do you decide whether to play left or right handed on a particular day?" He replied, "I take a look at which side my wife is sleeping on when I get up and that's the hand I play that day."

"But what happens if she is on her back?" one player asked, "Then I'm a bit late for the game!" he replied.

Playing a round of golf one day, Bill hit a shot into the middle of a field of buttercups.

As he was preparing to hit his next shot (probably uprooting most of the buttercups) a voice out of nowhere said, "Please don't hurt my buttercups." Bill, not sure he heard correctly, prepared to hit his shot anyway.

Again, a voice asked him not to hurt the buttercups. Bill placed his ball back on the fairway to make his shot and instantly MOTHER NATURE appeared. "Thank you for not hurting my buttercups. As a reward I will give you a year's supply of butter!" Bill was momentarily surprised and then he became angry ..... "Thanks a lot lady, but where were you when I was stuck in the PUSSY WILLOWS !!!"

The Pope met with his cardinals to discuss a proposal from Arial Sharon.

"Your Holiness" said one of the Cardinals, "Mr. Sharon wants to challenge you to a game of golf to show the friendship and ecumenical spirit shared by the Jewish and Catholic faiths."

The Pope thought it was a good idea, but he had never held a golf club in his life. "Have we not a cardinal," he asked, "who can represent me against the leader of Israel?" "None that plays golf very well," a cardinal said. "But," he added, "there is a man named Nick Faldo an English golfer who is a devout Catholic. We can offer to make him a cardinal; then ask him to play Mr Sharon as your personal representative.

In addition to showing our spirit of co-operation, we'll be sure to win the match." Everyone agreed it was a good idea. The call was made. Of course, Nick Faldo was honoured and agreed to play.

The day after the match, Faldo reported to the

Vatican to inform the Pope of the result. "I have some good news and some bad news, Your Holiness," said the world-class golfer. "Tell me the good news first," said the Pope. "Well, Your Holiness, I don't like to brag, but even though I've played some pretty terrific rounds of golf in my life, this was the best I have ever played, by far. I must have been inspired from above. My drives were long and true, my irons were accurate and my putting was perfect. With all due respect, my play was truly miraculous." "There's bad news?" the Pope asked. Faldo sighed. "I lost to Rabbi Woods by three strokes."

A young golfer was playing in his first PGA Tour event.

After his practice round he noticed a beautiful young lady by the clubhouse. He went up to her, began talking, and convinced her to come back to his hotel room for the night. All through the night they made wild love together. In the morning, the woman woke up and got out of bed. The man said, "Please don't go. I love you and I want you to stay with me." The woman replied, "You don't understand... I'm a hooker." The man said, "That's no problem, you probably just have too strong a grip."

An older couple are playing in the annual club championship.

They are playing a play-off hole and it is all down to a 6 inch putt that the wife has to make.

She takes her stance and her husband can see her trembling.

She putts and misses, they lose the match.

On the way home in the car her husband is fuming, "I can't believe you missed that putt!"

"That putt was no longer than my 'willy'," he said.

The wife just looked over at her husband and smiled and said, "Yes dear, but it was much harder!"

A man was golfing one day and was struck by lightning.

He died and went to heaven.

St Peter told him when he arrived at the gates of heaven that the bolt of lightning was actually meant for his golf partner.

But, because God doesn't want it known that he makes mistakes, the man would have to go back to earth as someone other that himself. Well, the man thought about it for a while and announced to Saint Peter that he wanted to return to earth as a lesbian. Saint Peter asked the man why a macho guy like him would choose to return as a lesbian.

The man answered, "It's simple really, this way I can still make love to a woman, AND I can hit from the red tees!! "

Husband and wife were playing in the mixed foursomes.

He hit a great drive down the middle - she sliced the second shot into a copse of trees. Unfazed he played a brilliant recovery shot which went onto the green a yard from the pin. She poked at the putt and sent it five yards beyond the pin.

He lined up the long putt and sank it.

To his wife he said, "We'll have to do better. That was a bogey five."

"Don't blame me," she snapped, "I only took two of them."

A golfer is on the second hole when he notices a frog sitting next to the green. He thinks nothing of it and is about to play when he hears, "Ribbit. 9 Iron" The man looks around and doesn't see anyone. "Ribbit. 9 Iron." He looks at the frog and decides to prove the frog wrong, puts his other club away, and grabs a 9 iron. Boom! he hits it 10 inches from the cup. He is shocked. He says to the frog, "Wow that's amazing. You must be a lucky frog, eh?" The frog reply's "Ribbit. Lucky frog." The man decides to take the frog with him to the next hole. "What do you think frog?" the man asks. "Ribbit. 3 wood." The guy takes out a 3 wood and Boom! Hole in one. The man is befuddled and doesn't know what to say. By the end of the day, the man golfed the best game of golf in his life and asks the frog, "OK where to next?" The frog replies, "Ribbit. Las Vegas." They go to Las Vegas and the guy says, "OK frog, now what?" The frog says, "Ribbit Roulette." Upon approaching the roulette table, the man asks, "What do you think I should bet?" The frog replies, "Ribbit. $3000, black 6." Now, this is a million-to-one shot to win, but after the golf game, the man figures what the heck. Boom! Tons of cash comes sliding back across the table. The man takes his winnings and buys the best room in the hotel. He sits the frog down and says, "Frog, I don't know how to repay you. You've won me all this money and I am forever grateful." The frog replies, "Ribbit, Kiss Me." He figures why not, since after all the frog did for him he deserves it.

With a kiss, the frog turns into a gorgeous 15-year-old girl. "And that, your honour, is how the girl ended up in my room."

A man and woman are at breakfast, she is having cup of coffee, he is reading the newspaper.

Wife to husband: "Honey, if I die before you, will you remarry?"

Husband, surprised, puts paper down and quietly replies: "Well, we have had a good marriage, and marriage is a good institution... so, yes, I'd probably remarry."

He goes back to reading the paper, she gets another cup of coffee and, after a few minutes, asks: "Honey, if I die before you, and you remarry, would you bring her to live in our house?"

He lowers the paper slowly, thinks for a second, and says, "Well, we worked hard to pay off the mortgage and it would be silly to move somewhere else so, yes, I think I would bring her to live here."

He returns to his paper, a few minutes passes and she asks: "Honey, if I die before you and you remarry and you bring her to live here in our house, would you let her use my golf clubs?" "Don't be ridiculous," he says as he slams down the paper, "She's a lefty."

A puzzled golfer watched a fellow member don some very unorthodox gear in the clubroom. "How long have you been wearing a corset?" he asked. "Ever since my wife found it in the car." was the reply.

Two men were out playing a game of golf. One of them was teeing off at the third hole, when a beautiful naked lady runs past. Naturally this distracted him, but the true committed golfer that he was, he resumed his stance.

As he was about to hit the shot again, two men in white coats ran past. "What's going on here?" he thought, once again taking his stance. Another distraction as a third man went running by in a white coat, but carrying two buckets of sand.

Eventually, he was ready again, and took his shot.

As he was walking down the fairway, he asked his companion what he thought had been going on.

His companion knew and told him: "Well that lady, once a week, manages to escape from the mental hospital beside the course, tears off her clothes and runs across the fairways. The three guys you saw were the nurses. They have a race to see which can catch her first, and the winner gets to carry her back."

"What about the buckets of sand?" "Well, that guy won last week, the buckets of sand are his handicap."

A big thunder storm hits a golf course and everyone runs for cover, except one man. He was asked afterwards why he didn't shelter from a dangerous lightning strike.

"No worries," he said. "I just take out my 1 iron and stand in the middle of the fairway with the club held high over my head and wait for the storm to pass.

Not even GOD can hit a 1 iron."

This Aussie bloke had been saving for years for the ultimate golfing holiday and finally he was off to the Royal Nairobi Golf & Country Club looking forward to the best game of his life.

He's allocated a personal caddie.

He thought it a bit unusual that the caddie had a shotgun but - hey, what the heck.

Off to the first tee he goes but he's so excited that his first shot slices off into the deep bush. You'll be OK, says his caddie, as he heads off into the bush with the shotgun looking for his ball. Then, all of a sudden, WHOOM.

Startled he turns around and sees the caddie with a huge smile on his face standing with one foot on this dead lion.

This is unbelievable he thinks and walks off to the next tee. But - he's a little shaken and he hits the ball off into the deep bush again.

His caddie once again walks into the bush. KATHUMPA!

The Aussie turns and there's his caddie again -

big smile on his face and his left foot on the head of a rhino. "No worries!" yells the caddie and they complete the hole.

Well the Aussie is a little bit shaken as he stands on the next tee contemplating the water hazard in front of him and - would you believe it - tops the ball into the water.

The caddie gives the thumbs up sign as he yells "You'll be able to get that, the water's shallow."

The Aussie is a little bit hesitant as he wades in, and for good reason.

Out of nowhere a huge alligator surges through the water, grabs his left leg and rips it off.

Surrounded by blood red water, he yells to the caddie "Why didn't you shoot him?' And the caddie yells back. "You don't get a shot on this hole!"

A young American golf fanatic decides to make the trip of a lifetime to Scotland, the Holy land of golf.

On his arrival he quickly heads out to the course and arranges a tee time.

Following his teaching pro's instructions, he requested and secured the best caddie the course had to offer: Olde Angus, the pride of the links for 53 years.

Happily the young American sets off on his dream round but 15 holes later numb and disgusted, 43 strokes over par, he reached over, grabbed his clubs and bag from Olde Angus and tossed them over the cliff into the churning sea below.

Turning to Angus he says, "You are positively the worst caddie on the face of this earth," to which Olde Angus replied "Nay, I dunna think that's possible laddie, it would be far too much of a coincidence."

Their regular foursome teed off on time that Saturday morning.

On the second hole Joe noticed a funeral procession going by and stopped, held his hat over his heart and bowed his head.

His partners noticed and complemented Joe on his thoughtfulness.

"She was a good wife for 40 years," replied Joe

St. Peter said "My friend," to the recently deceased, "you did lead an exemplary life on earth - but there is one instance of your taking the name of The Lord in vain. Would you care to tell us about it?"

"I recall," replied the new applicant, "it was in 1965 on the last hole at Wentworth. I only needed a par four to break 70 for the first time in my life." "Was your drive good?" asked St. Peter, with increasing interest. "Right down the middle," said the golfer. "But when I got to my ball, it was plugged deep in a wet rut made by a drunk's golf cart." "Oh dear," said St. Peter, "A real sucker! Is that when you..." "No. I'm pretty good with a 3-iron. I played the ball close to my feet, caught the sweet spot and landed it right on the green. But it bounced on a twig or something - it was a very windy day - and slid off the apron right under the steepest lip of the trap." "What a pity!" said St. Peter consolingly, "Then that must have been when..."

"No. I gritted my teeth, dug in with an open stance, swung a smooth outside arc, and backspun a bucket's worth of sand up onto the green. When everything settled down, there was my ball, only ten inches from the cup." "JESUS CHRIST!" shrieked St. Peter, "Don't tell me you choked the goddamn putt!"

A couple has a whirlwind, 30-day romance and even though they don't know too much about each other, they decide to get married. After a couple weeks, the husband says, "Honey, I have something I have to tell you. I'm a golf fanatic and I must play every day." "I also need to tell you something," she replies. "I'm a hooker, and I need to do it every day."

"That's OK," he said, "we'll just play dog leg lefts."

The husband and wife were playing on the 9th green when she collapsed from a heart attack. "Please dear, I need help." she said. The husband ran off saying "I'll go get some help."

A little while later he returned, picked up his club and began to line up his shot on the green.

His wife, on the ground, raised up her head and said, "I may be dying and you're putting?" "Don't worry, dear. I found a doctor on the second hole. He said he will come and help you."

"The second hole??? When in the world is he coming???"

"I told you not to worry," he said, practice stroking his putt.... "Everyone's already agreed to let him play through."

A man was stranded on a desert island for 10 years.

One day a beautiful girl swims to shore in a wet suit.

Man: "Hi. Am I ever happy to see you!"

Girl: "Hi. It seems like you've been here along time. How long has it been since you've had a cigarette?"

Man: "It has been ten years." With this information the girl unzips a slot on the arm of her wet suit and gives the man cigarette.

Man: "Oh thank you so much!"

Girl: "So tell me how long its been since you had a drink?"

Man: "It has been ten years." The girl unzips a little longer zipper on her wet suit and comes out with a flask of whisky and gives the man a drink.

Man: "Oh, thank you so much. You are like a miracle."

Finally, the girl starts to unzip the front of her wet suit and asks the man provocatively, "So tell me then, how long has it been since you played around?"

The man looked at her and said excitedly: "Oh, my God, don't tell me you've got a set of golf clubs in there, too?"

Three members of a foursome are standing in the fairway waiting for the fourth player to hit his ball.

While waiting, one guy asked another how his son was doing. The fellow replied, "Really great!! He is a car salesman and he sold so many cars last year that the dealership told him he could give a car to anyone he chose, and at no cost." "That's wonderful", said the first guy. "Sounds like my son who is a boat salesman. He sold so many that the dealer gave him a 19 foot speedboat to give away to anyone he wished." The third fellow chimed in, "That's amazing! My son sells apartments for a living and he also did so well last year that the developer told him he could give a 1 bedroom unit to anyone he liked."

About that time, the fourth member gets back to the fairway and joins his buddies. One asks, "John, how is your son doing ??" John replied, "Oh I'd rather not talk about him if you don't mind. I just found out that my son is gay." "Oh wow, that's a shame John", said the first golfer, "That must be Hell for you to deal with." "Well I guess it's not all bad" said John, "Just last month he received a free car, a free boat, and a free apartment!!"

One sunny spring day, there was a foursome of ladies at Cherry Hills Country Club about to play a par three, 165 yards long.
Quite suddenly, out from the trees beside the fairway, a streaker bounded across the open expanse of the fairway.
In a gasp, one of the women remarked, "Oh my! I think I know that guy. Isn't that Dick Green?" "No." replied her blonde golfing companion. "I think it's just a reflection from the grass."

In Scotland, a new game was invented. It was entitled Gentlemen Only Ladies Forbidden.... and thus the word GOLF entered the English language.

What's the difference between a G-Spot and a golf ball?
A man will actually search for a golf ball.

A lady golfer ran into the clubhouse screaming, "HELP, HELP! I've been stung by a bee and I'm allergic." The golf pro responded, "Where?" The lady answered, "Between the first and second hole!"

The pro stated, "You're stance is too wide."

You can order other Little books directly from Little Black Dog. All at relevant retail prices each including postage (UK only)

Postage and packing outside the UK: Europe: add 20% of retail price Rest of the world: add 30% of retail price

To order any book please call 01327 871 777

LITTLE **BLACK**DOG LIMITED 3 Everdon Park, Heartlands Business Park, Daventry NN11